Susan Evento &
Elizabeth Dana Jaffe

Design by Owen Design

Contributing Consultant
Dr. Robert W. Shumaker of
Great Ape Trust of Iowa

Meredith® Books
Des Moines, Iowa

THE WORLD'S
DEADLIEST
CREATURES

Discovery CHANNEL

D1160117

CONTENTS

4 POWERFUL AND POISONOUS

6 LION, CHEETAH, AND TIGER

8 POLAR BEAR AND GRIZZLY BEAR

10 CAPE BUFFALO

12 HIPPOPOTAMUS AND AFRICAN ELEPHANT

14 SPOTTED HYENA

16 GREAT WHITE SHARK, TIGER SHARK, AND BULL SHARK

18 NILE CROCODILE AND AMERICAN ALLIGATOR

20 KILLER BEES

22 BOMBARDIER BEETLE AND FIRE ANTS

24 SCORPION, FUNNEL-WEB SPIDER, AND REDBACK SPIDER

26 BOX JELLYFISH

28 STONEFISH AND CONE SHELL

30 PUFFERFISH AND BLUE-RINGED OCTOPUS

32 POISON DART FROG AND CANE TOAD

34 KOMODO DRAGON

36 GILA MONSTER

38 EASTERN DIAMONDBACK SNAKE AND KING COBRA

40 GLOSSARY

Deadly creatures are found all over the world—in deserts, jungles, caves, the tundra, and even the ocean! Some are big, like polar bears, tigers, and hippos. Others are small, like fire ants and beetles. No matter what their size, they all have deadly weapons! When they attack, it may be to get food or to defend themselves, their young, or their territory. Some use power or cunning to kill; others use poisons.

An animal's power might come from its size. An elephant, for example, can use its massive body to ram a lion threatening the elephant's calf. An animal's power might also come from its strength. With a single swat of its paw, a polar bear can take down prey. Other animals get their power from speed. A cheetah can run 70 mph over short distances.

Many animals deliver a deathblow with poison. Rattlesnakes use their fangs to pump poison into their prey. Killer bees use stingers to deliver their venom. And some poisonous creatures have unusual ways to defeat enemies: The bombardier beetle shoots poison through two "tailpipes" at the end of its abdomen!

Mammals, reptiles, insects, and even harmless-looking fish are among the world's deadliest creatures.

POWER

POI

Crocodile

ttlesnake

UL AND
SONOUS

LION

PROFILE
WEIGHT: 300 TO 500 POUNDS
BODY LENGTH: 6 TO 8 FEET
TAIL LENGTH: 3 FEET
SPEED: 35 MPH
HOME: AFRICA

The African lion is called the king of the beasts ... and for good reason. It is the top predator on the African savannah, weighing 500 pounds and measuring 8 feet in length when grown. The lion's body is built for hunting. Its back legs are for pouncing and propulsion and the front legs for grabbing and knocking down prey.

Lions hunt large to medium-size animals like the giraffe, zebra, wildebeest, and antelope. Female lions hunt in groups ... as if one wasn't powerful enough.

HOW THEY ATTACK!

The hunt begins with lions silently stalking their prey. When lions get within 100 feet, they charge. If the lions get close enough, they slap down or grab hold, knocking the prey to the ground. They then bite the mouth or throat to suffocate the animal.

CHEETAH

The cheetah is the fastest-moving land animal. Weighing about 140 pounds fully grown, cheetahs are slender, long-legged, and built for speed rather than fighting power. They can run 70 mph over short distances—the chase generally lasts about a minute, and if the cheetah doesn't catch the prey, it will give up rather than waste energy.

The cheetah is a carnivore, mostly eating the fast-moving gazelle. While the other big cats mainly hunt by night, the cheetah hunts early in the morning before it gets hot or later in the evening before dark.

HOW IT ATTACKS!

A cheetah does not hunt like other cats. Instead of using scent, it uses sight and speed to catch prey. Prey is stalked to within 100 feet, then chased down. The cheetah kills by tripping the animal, biting its throat, and suffocating it.

PROFILE
WEIGHT: 110 TO 140 POUNDS
BODY LENGTH: 3½ TO 4½ FEET
TAIL LENGTH: 3 FEET
SPEED: 70 MPH
HOME: AFRICA AND ASIA

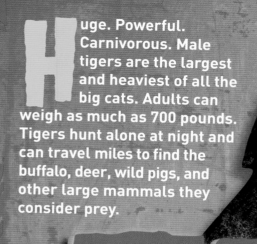

Huge. Powerful. Carnivorous. Male tigers are the largest and heaviest of all the big cats. Adults can weigh as much as 700 pounds. Tigers hunt alone at night and can travel miles to find the buffalo, deer, wild pigs, and other large mammals they consider prey.

HOW IT ATTACKS!

When it spots a tasty-looking animal in the forest, the tiger stalks it, moving slowly and silently, blending in with its environment. When the time is right, it pounces with lightning speed, tackling the creature with razor-sharp claws and a vicious mouth full of deadly teeth. The tiger's molars can cut through meat and muscle like a set of sharp knives working in unison. Its deadly canine teeth are the largest of any carnivorous land animal.

TIGER

TIGER EYES

In the dark, a tiger's eyesight is six times better than a human's.

PROFILE

WEIGHT: 200 TO 700 POUNDS
BODY LENGTH: 5 TO 10 FEET
TAIL LENGTH: 3 FEET
SPEED: 38 MPH
HOME: ASIA

HOW IT ATTACKS!

In the Arctic winter the temperature is about 30 degrees below zero! A hungry polar bear stands by a hole in the sheet of ice covering the sea, waiting for a seal to come up for air. The patient bear is prepared to wait hours. Suddenly, a seal appears and . . . swat! The polar bear hits the seal with its powerful front paw and pulls it up through the ice. Using sharp claws and teeth, the polar bear devours the entire seal, including blubber and skin.

POLAR BEAR

Standing up to 10 feet tall and weighing more than 1,300 pounds, polar bears are the largest of the land predators! These huge animals—one paw is 12 inches across—can run 30 mph for short distances and swim at least 50 miles.

The grizzly bear is one of the strongest animals in the world and one of the most dangerous. It can stand more than 8 feet tall and weigh more than 900 pounds. To an untrained eye, a grizzly may look big and slow. But don't be fooled! The grizzly can run 35 mph on all fours.

HOW IT ATTACKS!

A grizzly bear uses its sharp teeth and claws to catch prey such as squirrels, deer, birds, and fish. Its front paws throw powerful blows, which can break animals' necks or backs.

GRIZZLY BEAR

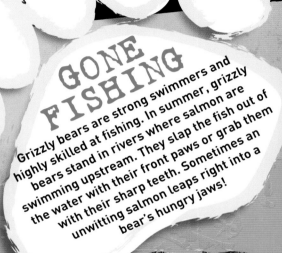

GONE FISHING

Grizzly bears are strong swimmers and highly skilled at fishing. In summer, grizzly bears stand in rivers where salmon are swimming upstream. They slap the fish out of the water with their front paws or grab them with their sharp teeth. Sometimes an unwitting salmon leaps right into a bear's hungry jaws!

PROFILE
WEIGHT: 300 TO 900 POUNDS
HEIGHT: 8 FEET
SPEED: 35 MPH
HOME: NORTH AMERICA, EASTERN AND WESTERN EUROPE, NORTHERN ASIA, AND JAPAN

The Cape buffalo is one of the most intimidating animals in Africa. Is it a vegetarian? It could be—it happens to like the taste of grass. Is it a predator? No, in fact, it is prey. A lion daring enough to attack a Cape buffalo, however, will be in for a real fight. In such situations, the lion often slinks away wounded instead of well-fed.

The adult Cape buffalo can grow to nearly 11 feet in length. It has a broad chest, short powerful legs, and a tail like a cow. Out of the sides of its large, heavy head, big ears covered with long fringes of hair droop downward. Massive horns begin at its forehead, forming a protective plate. The impressive horns curve down and then up into points—making them formidable weapons.

HOW IT ATTACKS!

The adult Cape buffalo, weighing in at about a ton, charges with astonishing speed and bashes into its enemies head and horns first. Then, if it needs to, it will come back for even more.

What a Deal!

Small birds, called oxpeckers, often perch on the Cape buffalo. They eat the fleas and ticks that live on the buffalo's hide. It sounds like a good deal because the oxpeckers get fed and the buffalo get cleaned! But be clear: Oxpeckers feed on the blood, so they also peck at the buffalo's sores to keep them open so more bugs will be attracted to the buffalo's hide.

E UFFALO

HIPPOPOTAMUS

Adult male Nile hippos can grow to be as big as 15 feet long and weigh 10,000 pounds. The hippo's skin grows to be more than an inch thick, which makes up 25 percent of its weight. As huge as hippos are, they can still run as fast as 30 mph. Hippos are plant-eaters that can consume as much as 150 pounds of food a day.

HOW IT ATTACKS!

Because hippopotamuses are plant-eaters, they do not hunt others. When annoyed or threatened, however, they can attack with the force of a tank. A crocodile threatening a calf will be charged, hit, and sent flying; a boat floating above an underwater hippo will be lifted out of the water and broken apart by these gigantic-size African mammals.

WHO NEEDS SUNSCREEN?

The hippopotamus has little body hair to protect its skin from the heat of the blazing African sun. To prevent its skin from drying out, a hippo stays in the water and covers itself with mud. The hippo's skin also secretes a red liquid that looks like blood—but acts like sunscreen.

AFRICAN ELEPHANT

THE NOSE KNOWS

The trunk is the elephant's most important tool. The trunk is a combination of the nose and upper lip, and it can weigh up to 300 pounds! Elephants use their trunks for drinking, bathing, trumpeting, eating, and, yes, fighting.

African elephants are extremely intelligent, caring creatures that are also the largest land mammals on the planet. An adult elephant eats as much as 500 pounds of plants, drinks 50 gallons of water, and walks 40 miles a day to feed—imagine what 10 elephants, each eating 500 pounds of plants, could do to a forest in a day.

HOW IT ATTACKS!

Despite its size, an African elephant is not a predator. However, when attacked or threatened the elephant spreads its ears to look even bigger and then charges. Being rammed by a charging elephant is like being hit by a moving truck. But being rammed is not the worst of it ... trampling comes next. An adult male elephant weighs in at 14,000 pounds; even one foot coming down would do serious damage to an attacker. Oh, and don't forget about the tusks. When not used for foraging and digging they come in handy when charging, ramming, and trampling don't quite finish the job.

PROFILE
WEIGHT: 3 TO 7 TONS
HEIGHT: 10 TO 13 FEET
SPEED: 25 MPH
HOME: AFRICA

13

Standing 3 feet tall and weighing up to 190 pounds, hyenas are surprisingly strong animals. Their muscular front legs and shoulders make them powerful killers. Their incredibly powerful jaws enable them to quickly crush and eat bones.

Hyenas are pack hunters—as many as 80 hyenas can be found in a clan or living group. Hunting together, they can overpower large animals such as zebras, gazelles, antelopes, impalas, wildebeests, Cape buffalo, and rhinos. Alone, a hyena will hunt small prey such as birds, lizards, snakes, and insects.

Due to their strength and cunning, hyenas have few predators—only people and lions. Hyenas and lions eat the same foods and often fight with one another over kills. Lions, which are much larger than hyenas, usually win those battles. But groups of hyenas can defeat lions if they outnumber the big cats.

HOW THEY ATTACK!

A pack of hyenas run toward a herd of animals and stop. They continue to do this until they spot one in the herd that is old, young, or sick, and chase just that animal. Hyenas run as fast as 30 mph and the chase can continue for miles. When the weak animal tires and can no longer run, the hyenas pull it to the ground with their large, sharp teeth. Hyenas eat fast—if they don't, more powerful predators may come along to steal dinner.

SPOTTED

LAUGHING HYENA

When threatened or excited, often when being chased, a hyena lets out a high sound like a cackle. It sounds like the hyena is laughing.

HYENA

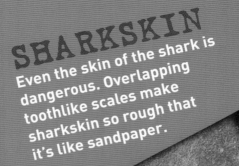

SHARKSKIN

Even the skin of the shark is dangerous. Overlapping toothlike scales make sharkskin so rough that it's like sandpaper.

PROFILE
WEIGHT: 2,500 TO 3,000 POUNDS
LENGTH: 15 TO 20 FEET
SPEED: 2 MPH
HOME: COASTAL WATERS, GREATEST CONCENTRATION ALONG SOUTH AFRICA

GREAT WHITE SHARK

The great white shark can be a whopping 20 feet long and weigh 3,000 pounds when grown. This shark has a massive appetite—it eats seals, sea turtles, porpoises, other sharks, and large fish. In fact, it eats anything it finds in its path. The great white shark is blamed for biting more humans than any other fish ... but it doesn't generally eat them.

HOW IT ATTACKS!

The great white shark usually attacks with a sudde burst of speed and a bite-and-spit movement that throws prey out of the water. The shark does this t protect itself from the claws or teeth of the wounded prey. The wounded prey is then circled until it is weak and then is eaten.

TIGER SHARK

PROFILE
WEIGHT: 2,200 POUNDS
LENGTH: 10 TO 18 FEET
SPEED: 3 MPH
HOME: WARM COASTLINES, BAYS, AND REEFS ALL OVER THE WORLD, EXCEPT THE CARIBBEAN

The tiger shark lives in tropical waters around the world. It likes to swim in the same warm, shallow waters where humans swim. Watch out! Unlike the great white shark, the tiger shark likes the taste of humans!

HOW IT ATTACKS!

As soon as this dangerous shark spots something that looks edible, it puts on a burst of speed, opens its powerful jaws, and bites down with razor-sharp teeth.

BULL SHARK

As it searches for prey in shallow coastal areas, this 10-foot-long, 500-pound shark moves slowly and lazily. Its attitude can quickly change. Highly aggressive and territorial, the bull shark is one of the most dangerous sharks in the world.

HOW IT ATTACKS!

When a bull shark locates a potential meal—such as a dolphin—it picks up speed, zipping through the water at 20 mph in short bursts. At speed, the bull shark gives the surprised victim a powerful shove with its short, blunt snout. Then the bull shark strikes again, this time sinking sharp, inch-long teeth into its prey.

PROFILE
WEIGHT: 200 TO 500 POUNDS
LENGTH: 7 TO 10 FEET
SPEED: 3 MPH
HOME: TROPICAL AND TEMPERATE WATERS, SHALLOW COASTAL WATERS

The Nile crocodile is one of the largest reptiles on Earth and an extremely dangerous predator. It can be found in rivers, freshwater marshes, or lakes. A Nile crocodile can grow to be 18 feet long and weigh 2,000 pounds. It eats buffalo, warthogs, hyenas, baboons, antelope, fish, and birds.

HOW IT ATTACKS!

The Nile crocodile lies and waits for the right moment. When prey is spotted, it moves slowly and quietly just under the surface of the water with only its eyes showing. When prey is within reach, the crocodile lunges out of the river and grabs the prey in its powerful jaws. Finally, it drags its victim underwater and drowns it.

NILE CROCODILE

American alligators are the largest reptiles in North America, growing to 15 feet in length and weighing 1,000 pounds at maturity. They inhabit freshwater and brackish (slightly salty) swamps, marshes, canals, and lakes.

An alligator is mostly carnivorous, eating fish, frogs, turtles, snakes, raccoons, deer, and other small alligators. It's not too picky, though, as it will also swallow sticks and aluminum cans! It has been known to snack on dogs and cats too—and the occasional human of course.

HOW IT ATTACKS!

An American alligator hunts in the water at night. It swims quickly, mainly using its tail and webbed feet to propel itself.

As it swims it snaps up small prey with its jaws and swallows it whole. An alligator also uses its jaws to drag large prey underwater and drown it.

AMERICAN ALLIGATOR

PROFILE

WEIGHT: 1,000 POUNDS

LENGTH: 10 TO 15 FEET

SPEED: KNOWN FOR SUDDEN BURSTS OF SPEED

HOME: SOUTHEASTERN UNITED STATES

KILLER

PROFILE
WEIGHT: A TENTH OF A GRAM
LENGTH: ½ INCH
SPEED: 20 MPH
HOME: CENTRAL AND SOUTH AMERICA, SOUTHERN UNITED STATES

KILLER BEE

HONEYBEE

DYING TO STING

Only worker bees sting—and when they do, the stinger and the attached venom sac get stuck in the victim. Typically, once a bee loses its stinger, it dies within an hour.

BEES

Killer bees, also called Africanized honeybees, have not always been around. In 1956, a university professor wanted to breed a new kind of honeybee that would make more honey. The professor brought 63 African queen honeybees to Brazil for an experiment. Some of the bees escaped and bred with the local honeybees. This created a new type of bee that was quicker to attack and more likely to swarm than regular honeybees—killer bees were born!

Killer bees soon took over the hives of local honeybees. They spread throughout South and Central America and the southern United States. Today they continue to spread northward.

HOW THEY ATTACK!

Killer bees are territorial and go on a rampage if they feel their hive or nest is being threatened. Like regular honeybees, killer bees have venomous stingers that they use to inject poison into their victims. The stinger is like a needle, shaped like a fishhook, with a venom-filled sac attached. A single sting won't kill, but killer bees attack in a swarm. Some victims are stung up to 500 times. This large number of stings can seriously injure or kill a victim.

IN CASE OF ATTACK

Fortunately, attacks by killer bees are rare. But if attacked, run and get inside a sheltered area. If you are stung several times, get to a hospital.

Bombardier beetles, which are found on most continents, are social creatures. They look for food during the day, but otherwise gather in dark, damp places like logs.

HOW IT ATTACKS!

When attacked, the bombardier beetle has a built-in weapon. The beetle's body mixes two chemicals into a poison that is boiling hot—212°F! The beetle shoots the super-heated poison at the attacker through two "tailpipes" on its abdomen. The beetle can turn its abdomen almost in a complete circle without moving its legs, to the position of its predator, giving it excellent aim. The poison makes a popping sound as it blasts out of the beetle. For the beetle's enemy, the result may be blindness or death. On human skin the poison feels like a painful burn.

A bombardier beetle can rapidly shoot its poison up to 29 times in a row; the spray can travel a distance up to four times its body length.

BOMBARDIER BEETLE

PROFILE

WEIGHT: .10 GRAMS
LENGTH: ½ INCH
SPEED: 0.3 MPH
HOME: MOST CONTINENTS AROUND THE WORLD

FIRE ANTS

It can be difficult to tell fire ants from other ants up until they bite and sting. A fire ant, like any insect, has a body that is divided into three separate sections: head, thorax, and abdomen. It has a copper-color head and body, three pairs of legs, and a pair of antennae.

HOW THEY ATTACK!

The attack starts when fire ants swarm over the victim. The first ant to sting releases a chemical that signals the other ants to sting. The ant starts by biting the victim's skin with tiny but powerful jaws. Once the jaw is locked in place, the ant uses its abdominal stinger to inject venom, causing a painful burning sensation and blisters. Each ant stings repeatedly, turning its abdomen to sting in a circle.

VICIOUS VENOM

The fire ant's venom can paralyze insects and lizards, but larger animals have died from fire ant stings. If you are stung, wash the affected area with soap and water. If you're allergic to insect venom, seek medical help immediately!

SCORPION

PROFILE
WEIGHT: 30 GRAMS
LENGTH: 2½ TO 7½ INCHES
HOME: MOST CONTINENTS

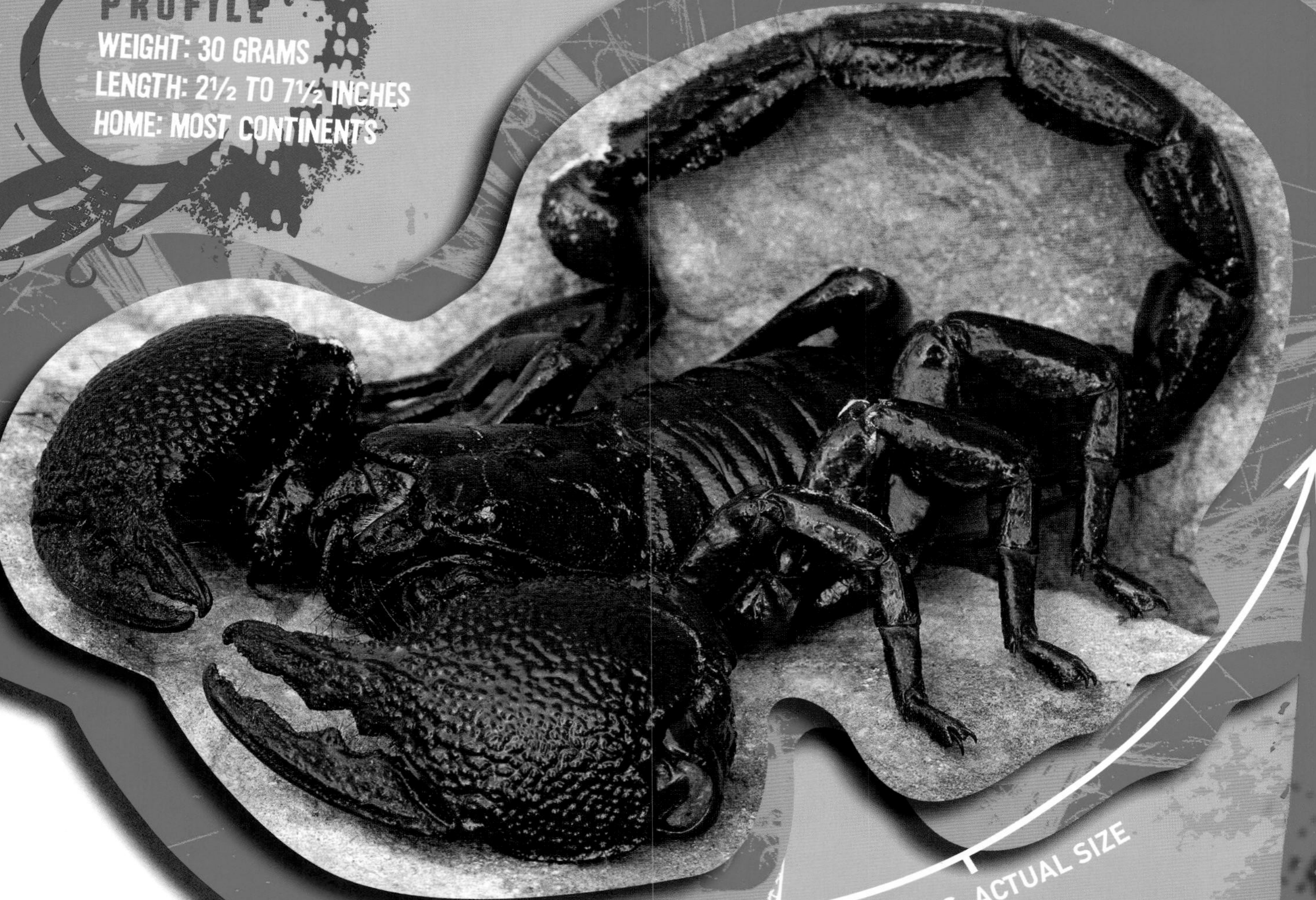

7½ INCHES–ACTUAL SIZE

The body of a scorpion is divided into two parts: the head and abdomen. The cephalothorax, or the head, is where to find the eyes, mouth, claws, and three or four pairs of legs. The abdomen is covered with plates like a knight in armor with a venom-filled stinger.

Scorpions are carnivores that hunt spiders, beetles, lizards, and other scorpions. Although their sting is painful to humans, it doesn't usually cause serious harm.

HOW IT ATTACKS!

Snap! The scorpion grabs with its claws, then arches its tail over its back and jabs its stinger into its prey. The scorpion then rocks its tail to work the stinger in even deeper. Finally, it injects its victim with deadly venom.

The funnel-web spider is large with a shiny dark brown carapace, or shell, covering the front part of the body. The fangs point straight down and drip with venom when it is about to strike.

HOW IT ATTACKS!

The spider's funnel-shape web leads into its burrow. Silk strands also lead away from the web. The spider waits until prey trips over a strand of the web. Feeling the vibration, the spider attacks with huge, venom-dripping fangs.

FUNNEL-WEB SPIDER

PROFILE
LENGTH: 1/2 TO 2 INCHES
SPEED: LESS THAN 1 MPH
HOME: AUSTRALIA

BIG ENOUGH TO BITE?

Only female redback spiders are big enough to bite humans. The venom causes vomiting and convulsions. Get antivenin if you are bitten.

REDBACK SPIDER

PROFILE
LENGTH: 1½ TO 4 INCHES
SPEED: LESS THAN 1 MPH
HOME: AUSTRALIA

Redback spiders are black with a red stripe on the upper abdomen and a red spot on the underside. The spider's body is about the size of a pea with long slender legs.

HOW IT ATTACKS!

Redback spiders lurk in funnel-shape webs, waiting for prey to get stuck. The redback quickly wraps prey in silk while stunning it with its venomous bite, then sucks out the prey's juices.

25

DEAD YET DANGEROUS

A box jellyfish is dangerous even when dead! If you find one washed ashore, don't touch its tentacles, even if they are dry. For a short time after it dies, the tentacles can sting anything that touches them.

BOX JELLYFISH

The box jellyfish is actually bell shaped and has four sides like a box. Fully grown, its body is about 10 inches across. A box jellyfish has 60 tentacles that are each 3 yards long and hang from the corners of its transparent body. The box jellyfish moves through the water at 3 mph eating shrimp and small fish.

HOW IT ATTACKS!

The box jellyfish is one of the most dangerous creatures in the sea. The surface of each of its tentacles is packed with thousands of tiny stinging cells. When the hairs on these cells are touched, the cells shoot tiny harpoons filled with powerful poison. Just one tentacle can shoot enough poison to cause dangerous burns and often a painful death within a matter of minutes.

WATCH YOUR STEP!

Because stonefish are so well camouflaged, a person may accidentally step on them. Their sharp spines can cut through a sneaker, and venom is injected into the person's foot. The venom causes intense pain and affects the lungs and heart. Antivenin, medicine that offsets the effects of poison, must be injected into the victim within a couple of hours to prevent death.

Tail

Mout

The stonefish is the most venomous fish in the world. This carnivorous, 12-inch-long, wart-covered, multicolored fish has a face only a mother could love. The colors and bumps all over its body help the stonefish blend in with the coral and rocks in tropical ocean water where it lives and hunts.

STONEFISH

HOW IT ATTACKS!

A stonefish hunts fish and crustaceans by blending in with surrounding rocks or burying itself in the sand and waiting for prey to swim past. Then it attacks, seemingly from out of nowhere, with incredible speed.

To protect itself the stonefish has 13 thick, sharp spines along its back. Attached to each spine is a pair of small venom sacs. When a predator, such as a shark or stingray, touches its spines, the stonefish releases its poison.

PROFILE

WEIGHT: LESS THAN 2 POUNDS
LENGTH: 12 INCHES
SPEED: MOTIONLESS, UNLESS ATTACKING
HOME: PACIFIC AND INDIAN OCEANS

Cone shells are small mollusks with beautiful shells. They can grow to 10 inches long, but most are much smaller. The creatures are so small, prey doesn't even know a cone shell is there until it becomes dinner. There are 500 different species of cone shells and all of them are poisonous—some are deadly. All cone shells are carnivorous and eat marine worms, small fish, mollusks, and other cone shells.

CONE SHELL

HOW IT ATTACKS!

Cone shells are slow-moving creatures, so they use venom-filled harpoons covered with barbs to spear fast-moving prey. When prey passes by, the harpoon is shot like a dart and the poison is injected. Prey quickly becomes paralyzed and the cone shell uses the harpoon to reel in the prey and eat it. The venom of some types of cone shell is powerful enough to kill a human.

PRIZED POSSESIONS

Cone shells are beautiful as well as deadly. These patterned shells are highly prized by collectors. If you see a cone-shaped shell the next time you are at the beach, you might want to think twice about picking it up!

PUFFERFISH

Pufferfish are carnivores that range in size from 1 inch to 2 feet in length. They have four teeth that, when pressed together, form what looks like a beak. They use these to crush the shells of crustaceans and mollusks. The body of a pufferfish is covered with spikes that lay flat against its body.

JAPANESE DELICACY

Japanese prepare a dish made from pufferfish called *fugu*. Although chefs carefully remove the poisonous parts, people sometimes still become ill. There is no antidote.

PROFILE
WEIGHT: LESS THAN 4 LBS
LENGTH: UP TO 24 INCHES
SPEED: WHEN PUFFED UP, HALF OF ITS NORMAL SPEED
HOME: SUBTROPICAL AND TROPICAL WATERS IN THE ATLANTIC, PACIFIC, AND INDIAN OCEANS

HOW IT ATTACKS!

When a predator attacks, the pufferfish swallows water and blows up like a balloon, making it three times its normal size. The once-flat spikes stand up so it's impossible for a predator to swallow it. The internal organs of many pufferfish are full of poison, so if a predator swallows it, the predator probably dies. There is enough poison in one pufferfish to kill 30 people!

BLUE-RINGED OCTOPUS

The blue-ringed octopus' body is about the size of a golf ball with eight 4-inch-long tentacles. The octopus camouflages itself to hunt and hide from predators, but when an attacker comes, it turns bright yellow with blue rings. It hunts small crabs, hermit crabs, shrimp, and fish if it can catch them. The octopus will bite an attacker—it has enough poison to kill 26 humans in minutes.

HOW IT ATTACKS!

Usually the blue-ringed octopus minds its own business, feeding on hermit crabs. But when it's threatened, its dull color turns brighter and its blue rings flash, advising intruders to get lost. If the warning is ignored, the octopus uses sharp jaws to inject its poison. The poison immediately paralyzes the victim and can lead to heart failure. There is no antivenin.

31

Many poison dart frogs are small with brightly colored skin. The skin color can run from orange and black to blue or yellow but most are brown. The largest of the poison dart frogs can grow to be 2½ inches long.

HOW IT ATTACKS!

A poison dart frog's body secretes poison. Some predators are immune to the poison's effects. But most would-be attackers feel the effects immediately when they touch or try to eat the frog. In fact, the poison from one frog is so powerful it can kill many humans! The poison attacks nerve and muscle cells, sometimes causing heart failure and death.

POISON DART FROG

PROFILE
WEIGHT: 3 GRAMS
LENGTH: 1 TO 2½ INCHES
HOME: RAIN FORESTS OF CENTRAL AND SOUTH AMERICA

CANE TOAD

Adult cane toads can grow to 15 inches long and weigh as much as 5 pounds. They're capable of sucking air into their lungs and lifting their bodies off the ground to look bigger to an attacker. Adult cane toads have large glands behind their eyes and across their backs. When they are attacked, they ooze a toxic, milky liquid. Cane toads eat whatever they can swallow, but feed mostly on beetles, termites, honeybees, ants, and crickets.

HOW IT ATTACKS!

When the cane toad is attacked, it turns on its side so its glands are aimed at the predator. The poison oozes out, but toads can also spray the poison. All the poison has to do is get into the eyes, nose, or mouth of the predator to work. Cane toad attacks are sometimes fatal.

PROFILE

WEIGHT: 5 POUNDS
LENGTH: 4 TO 9 INCHES
HOME: NORTH AND SOUTH AMERICA AND AUSTRALIA

FAST FACT

Even this toad's eggs and tadpoles are poisonous, but strangely, just after turning from tadpole to frog it is not all that dangerous ... for a little while!

33

KOMODO

The Komodo dragon lives on four hot, dry islands in Indonesia. It is the world's largest and heaviest living lizard. It may grow 10 feet long and weigh more than 200 pounds. The Komodo dragon is carnivorous and has an appetite that matches its size. It will eat more than 150 pounds of food at one time.

The Komodo hunts pigs, deer, boar, snakes, water buffalo, rats, and other Komodo dragons! It's also been known to kill people. The dragon has a flexible skull, which allows it to swallow large pieces of food. It eats every part of an animal, including the fur and bones.

HOW IT ATTACKS!

The Komodo dragon smells with its tongue. It finds the scent of its prey and waits in hiding. When prey approaches, the Komodo lunges and chases it down, then bites, releasing poisonous bacteria from its mouth into the wound. The prey may get away, but it's only a matter of time until the bacteria causes an infection. The prey dies in a few days. The dragon finds the now-dead prey by its scent, even if it's 2½ miles away!

STINKY BREATH

The Komodo dragon has foul breath because its mouth is full of harmful bacteria.

PROFILE

WEIGHT: 150 TO 200 POUNDS
LENGTH: 8 TO 10 FEET
SPEED: 11 MPH
HOME: INDONESIAN ISLANDS

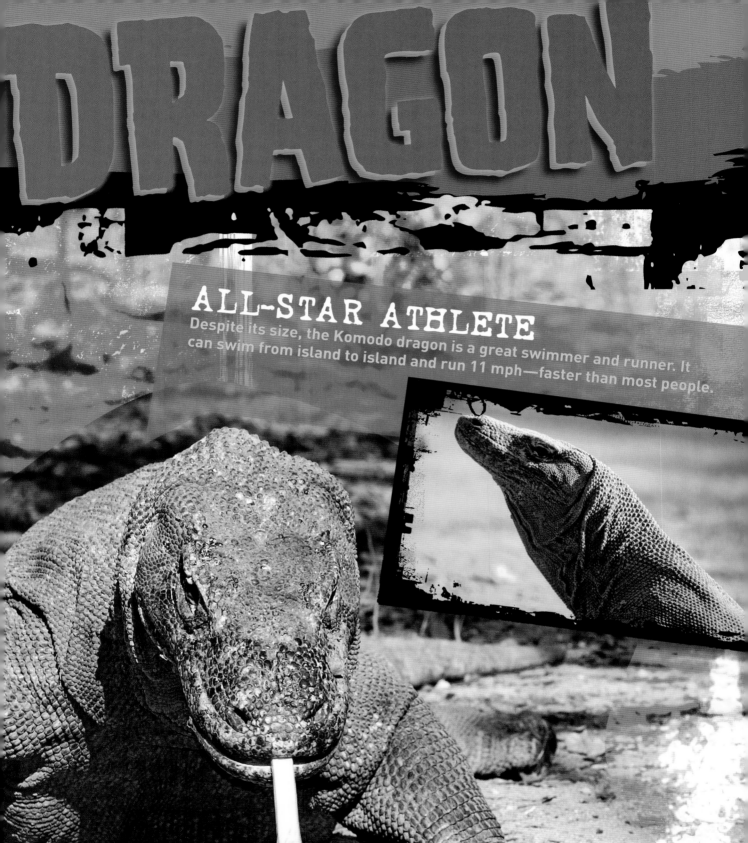

DRAGON

ALL-STAR ATHLETE

Despite its size, the Komodo dragon is a great swimmer and runner. It can swim from island to island and run 11 mph—faster than most people.

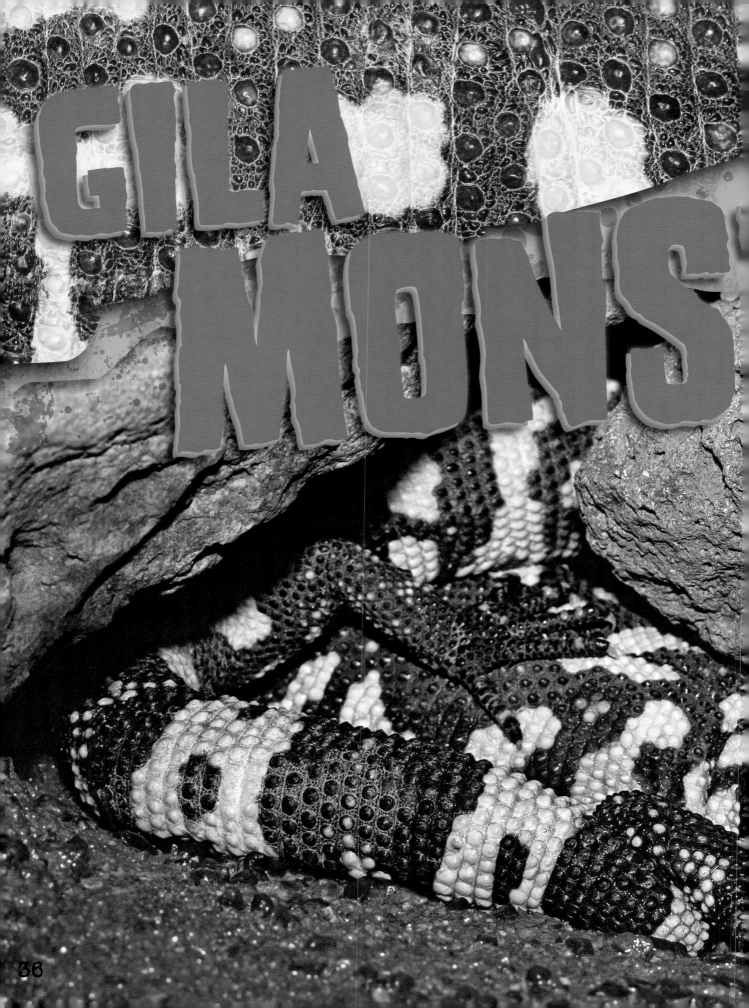

GILA MONS

ER T

The Gila monster grows to be 2 feet long and weigh 5 pounds as an adult. It is a slow lizard with beadlike scaly skin that is black, yellow, pink, and orange. The bright colors warn predators that it is poisonous. The Gila monster rests most of the time and lives alone in a burrow. When a Gila monster does come out to feed, it hunts for eggs, birds, and squirrels. It has a thick, short tail that is full of fat that the lizard can live off of when there is no food or it is hibernating.

HOW IT ATTACKS!

The Gila monster hunts primarily with its senses of taste and smell instead of its eyes. It smells its prey and tracks it down by flicking its tongue to taste the smell left behind. Since it must grab its prey with its jaws, surprise is important. After clamping its jaws on its victim, its grooved teeth fill up with poison produced by glands in its mouth. It cannot inject venom into the victim. Instead it must use its teeth to grind the venom into the wound.

The Gila monster doesn't need to use its poison on small prey—its bite is strong enough for that. Some scientists believe that the Gila monster's venom is used for protection.

DID YOU KNOW?

Each "bead" on the skin of a Gila monster has an osteoderm—a tiny round piece of bone.

PROFILE
WEIGHT: 5 POUNDS
LENGTH: 1½ TO 2 FEET
SPEED: CONSIDERED SLOW, EXCEPT WHEN IN DEFENSE MODE
HOME: UNITED STATES

SHAKE, RATTLE, AND GROW
Every time a rattlesnake sheds its skin, its rattle adds a new interlocking segment.

PROFILE
WEIGHT: 15 TO 23 POUNDS
LENGTH: 7 FEET
SPEED: 3 MPH
HOME: NORTH AMERICA, CENTRAL AMERICA, AND SOUTH AMERICA

The eastern diamondback has a triangular-shape head and rattles at the end of its tail, which it shakes to warn others away. The eastern diamondback is the largest species of rattlesnake—responsible for most of the snakebite deaths in North America—growing as long as 7 feet.

There are 28 species of rattlesnakes, living in all types of habitats.

HOW IT ATTACKS!

The eastern diamondback hunts or hides and waits for prey. It can't see its prey, but the heat-sensitive pit on the side of its face tells it prey is nearby. When it attacks the snake lunges forward, sinking its fangs into its prey. The fangs release poison into the bloodstream, killing small prey instantly. Larger prey is bitten and released—the poison takes about 30 minutes to kill—then the diamondback follows the scent trail to its dinner.

The diamondback's prey includes rabbits, squirrels, rats, and birds. To eat, it unhinges its jaw and swallows its prey whole, headfirst. Rattlesnakes avoid people, but they will attack if threatened. Their bite can be deadly; antivenin is available.

EASTERN DIAMONDBACK RATTLESNAKE

KING COBRA

The king cobra is the largest venomous land snake in the world! It can grow to 18 feet long and weigh as much as 20 pounds. The king cobra eats mostly other snakes. After a large meal, however, it may go for months without eating.

PROFILE
WEIGHT: 13 TO 20 POUNDS
LENGTH: 13 TO 18 FEET
SPEED: 3 MPH
HOME: SOUTHEAST ASIA AND INDIA

HOW IT ATTACKS!

Like other snakes, the king cobra smells with its tongue. When it finds the scent of prey, the king cobra flicks its tongue, feels the vibrations of the prey's movements, and uses its powerful eyesight—it can see more than 300 feet—to locate the prey.

A king cobra bites into its prey, forcing venom through fangs into the wound. One bite can deliver enough venom to kill an elephant! Following the bite, it will begin to swallow its prey whole (headfirst)—and alive. The cobra's jaw is attached, but it is stretchy so the cobra can swallow prey that is wider than its own head.

HOME BUILDERS
Cobras are the only snakes that build nests for their eggs, protecting the nests closely until the eggs hatch safely.

GLOSSARY

Ambush: a surprise attack

Antivenin: a medicine that offsets the effects of poison

Carnivore: a creature that eats meat

Clan: group of animals

Crustacean: an animal living in the water that has a skeleton around the outside of its body

Gram: a unit of weight equal to one thousandth of a kilogram, the weight of a U.S. dollar bill

Herd: a group of animals that lives together

Ounce: a measure of weight equal to one-sixteenth of a pound

Paralyze: to make unable to move

Poison: a substance that can cause injury or death

Predator: an animal that hunts another animal for food

Prey: an animal that another animal hunts for food

Pride: a group of lions that lives together

Stalk: to hunt another animal in a slow and quiet way

Stinger: a part of an animal that is sharp and pointed that can pierce or wound and inject poison

Swarm: bees or other insects that move in a group

Ton: a unit of weight equal to 2,000 pounds

Venom: the poison of some animals, such as snakes and spiders, that can be passed to prey or a victim through a bite or sting

Victim: someone or something that is harmed or killed